GOLF

Too Many Swing Thoughts

by

Larry Eichenauer

Published by
Heritage Publishing.US
Bradenton, Florida
www.heritagepublishingus.com

Contents

Foreword

Nearly all professional golfers started golfing at a young age with the assistance of professional instruction. They acquired their talent without the misfortune of swing faults that often seem impossible to correct. You would think, since it takes just 1-2 seconds to complete a golf swing, it should not be a difficult feat. But for some reason, 90 percent of all golfers are lucky to shoot less than 90 on a normal course using the shorter tee boxes. Over the past 25 years, with all the advancements in equipment, golf balls, slow motion video, many more instructors, and YouTube, the average score among this same group of golfers has not improved. So, you have to ask yourself, "why"? This is the reason I have chosen to write this book. It is my goal to answer this question by providing an amateur's perspective that has been overlooked by most professionals. What is not being recognized with modern golf instruction is that the modern golf swing requires more mental training than physical training.

In the early beginnings, the game of golf was not a methodical sport. During this era, golf was played with carved wooden clubs and a feather stuffed ball. The ball was struck with a carefree swing, having little thought for how the body should twist and turn to get this strange ball into a hole with the least amount of strokes.

Fast forward to present day. We now have refined equipment, practice ranges, golf instructors, and exquisite well manicured golf courses. Everything about the game has become so precise that we may have gone too far. Technology has led the way to encourage this desire for perfection. It is promoted that we must swing a certain way if you choose to succeed at golf. In reality, swinging a golf club, should be, as natural as swinging a baseball bat. I believe the golf swing needs to be more the result of a reflex action rather than a prescribed action.

Before writing this, I spent years trying to learn a prescribed way with countless swing thoughts. There is a right and wrong way to swing a golf club but, it must eventually feel natural. Several chapters in this book provide an in-depth look at how the professionals swing, followed by recommendations to help amateurs learn how to perform at a higher level.

We need to look closely at how we train our mind and body if we want to change the statistics that 90% of all golfers continue to shot over 90. In this book, I will make suggestions for how to improve these numbers. Golf instruction needs to concentrate more on motor skill training, rather than allowing the brain to be filled with "too many swing thoughts".

Chapter 1

Too Many Swing Thoughts

"You swing your best when you have the fewest things to think about."

Bobby Jones

"Success depends almost entirely on how effectively you learn to manage the games two ultimate adversities: the course and yourself."

Jack Nicklaus

I can't think of a better place to start than by referencing my first golf outing with my wife. This would have been many years ago, prior to my golf addiction and acquired knowledge of the golf swing. Before taking lessons from a professional instructor, my wife's only experience with golf was a nearby putt-putt facility. I suggested lessons before going out on the course. She started with five lessons. As a beginner, it can be overwhelming so all the sessions were about learning the basics. After completing the series of lessons, she accomplished far more than I had expected. Her setup looked impressive and her swing was not that bad. So now, it's time to take it to the course. I chose a par 3 course for our first golf outing. It took no more than two holes to realize I had to keep my mouth shut. Her mind was so overwhelmed with swing thoughts, such as head down, arm straight, and focus on the ball, I soon learned you do not make suggestions unless it's requested. After our first experience on the course, she said she had fun, but I could tell she didn't enjoy golf like I did. The saturation of "too many swing thoughts" was enough to take most of the fun out of the game. This can be a problem for so many amateurs. Swing thoughts produce so much tension that the average golfer is unable to play golf just for fun. Unlike other sports, there is that lack of freedom to just let go and enjoy the moment.

For the amateur, it is difficult to stand over a golf ball and not think about all of the golf moves you have been practicing. If a child is shown a video, or is able to watch a professional golfer swing a club, they can nearly duplicate the correct swing. They are not thinking about anything except trying to copy what they saw. If we could continue this innocent approach to golf as an adult we would all be more natural golfers. For some reason, as we age we want to be in control. If the golf ball were moving instead of just sitting there waiting to be struck, we could stop our minds from diverting to the control mode. Most professional golfers were taught or learned the correct way to swing a golf club at a young innocent age, making their golf swing a more natural process.

The problem with golf is that the stationary ball somehow makes the average adult want to think how to send the ball to the target by managing the way they swing. Our brain is structured wherein the left brain is the thinking and reasoning side, and the right brain is the more visual and creative side. You could say that the right side of the brain is more favorable for sports. If a swing thought is used while swinging a golf club, you are trying to control the action with the left part of the brain instead of the right. This act will cause confession in the right side and produce unpredictable results. This would be like telling your arm how to move when throwing a ball. You have performed this action without thought since you can remember. The right brain performs activities better without too much information. It's the reason why you practice something over and over until you no longer have to think about it. When a player is said to be "in the zone" all their actions are on auto-pilot and as a result, they play the best golf of their lives.

Since the downswing happens in less than a quarter second, it is hard to imagine how swing thoughts could be used successfully. That is the point, they can't. If you use swing "feels" it might be possible to influence some part of a downswing. Even ONE swing feel is difficult for most golfers. The problem with swing thoughts while swinging is that they inhibit natural flow, which produces tension. Tension will affect the swing in so many ways.

Is there a difference between swing "thoughts" and swing "feels"? A swing feel is typically less invasive. A swing feel is sensing a process that is just part of an action. Whereas, a swing thought is thinking about a position or movement of a body part. An example of a swing feel would be sensing (feeling) your belt buckle moving toward the target at the end of your swing. You are not telling your body to move. You are feeling that it is just going to happen without forcing it. A swing thought would be, "move the right elbow to your right side at the beginning of the downswing". This requires the left brain to tell the right brain what to do. A better way to perform this action would be to feel like the right arm is skipping a stone. This would be more of an action that the right brain can relate to. This is why most golf instructors try to use swing feels to produce an action. It is a matter of semantics. Most instructors use the term "swing through" the impact area, rather than "hit" the ball. This can produce different results just by using different words to reference a similar action. "Hit" is placing too much emphasis on the ball, making golfers start the downswing too aggressively from the top.

How about using swing thoughts or feels during the backswing? A backswing normally takes 3 times longer than the downswing. Some golfers have backswings that take more than a second. Most people would say: "That's enough time for two or three swing thoughts". Again, when the body and club are moving, any STRAY thoughts will produce tension by trying to take control of a movement. Over the years I have tried a variety of swing thoughts and feels, and I have found so few that will work without wrecking the swing. I eventually discovered that swing thoughts having to do with body part movements are the problem. Swing thoughts that relate to a fairly stationary position can work. For example, if you are trying to prevent sway in a backswing, you can think about keeping your upper body and head more "centered" over the ball. This prevents swaying and no movement was suggested by the left brain. The left side of the brain can suggest something without movement and not affect the ability for the right side of the brain to complete the flow of the swing. This brings up the thought about keeping your head still, which is actually important for producing a consistent swing. The problem with this swing thought, it becomes TOO restrictive. Most instructors avoid this thought just like I mentioned the word "hit". Most would prefer not using the head as a stationary point because it can reduce how you turn back and through the impact zone. Most instructors will use "staying more centered, chest facing the ball, proper shoulder turn", etc. In other words, if you're using a swing thought that relates to being very stationary, don't use that type of swing thought. Every part of your body moves during a golf swing. Rigidity is never a term for swinging a golf club. Sam Snead would reference his swing as being "oily". His swing was as smooth as it gets. If you want a swing thought, think "oily". I believe that you need to be creative in your choice of words when it comes to swing thoughts. It may really help prevent tension.

One universal thought is "keep your eyes on the ball". This is widely used, and since this is your immediate target, it is very important that you use this swing thought for all shots. Jack Nicklaus said he looked down at the ball, but in his mind it was "just there". He saw the ball as a whole. This would be the way you would visualize a baseball as you see it coming towards you before you swing away with a bat. You would see a ball thrown to you in the same way. Some golfers look at a spot, marking, or dimple on the ball. A few golfers, for iron play focus on a spot in the grass a couple inches in front of the ball. They say looking ahead helps them swing through the ball for better compression. All these methods are fine, as long as the focus does not become fixated, which makes you lose focus on the real target (a spot in the fairway or green). Fixated is just another word for tension. I prefer the Jack Nicklaus approach because it is more subconscious, just like trying to catch a ball. "It's just there".

I must emphasize that using swing thoughts is fine when you practice. How else does one learn the correct way to swing? Some swing thoughts may work for one person, but not another. Some swing thoughts work one day, and the next day, they don't. It is important to experiment. Some of the best swing thoughts relate to other activities. For example, throwing a Frisbee with your left hand (right hand golfers) is similar to the action of the left arm and wrist near impact and follow-through.

This really improves follow-through, so don't hesitate to toss a Frisbee now and then. Another, is "skipping a stone". This is a great right arm swing thought, and great to use when practicing. Making a side arm throw is another thought. These actions can really improve the movement of the right elbow. Watch professional golfers in slow motion and you can see the similarity to these activities.

I cannot stress enough the importance of this chapter. I spent years using every swing thought you could imagine and got caught in the viscous cycle of thinking, "I finally got it", to discover that was not the case. What may work one time, would not work the next. Even the pros use some swing thoughts when the game is not up to their standards. Some people that are already good golfers can actually use swing thoughts on the course. But I am certain, they use only one at a time and it is not continuous. Like in all sports, you have days when you can do nothing wrong. Then, there are those days when you can't do anything right. Amateurs should try to avoid swing thoughts on the golf course. Unless you are a professional it will not work. I can attest to this problem. It took five years to stop playing "golf swing" instead of just playing "golf". I will tell you that there is a 99 percent chance you will not improve at golf if you continue down the road of swing thoughts WHEN ON

THE GOLF COURSE. If you want to go to the course and play by yourself to experiment, and treat your time there as just practice, that is okay. But you would be better off just practicing at home or on the range.

This brings up the topic of how to practice. If I could go back in time, when I set the goal to "swing like a pro", I would change my procedure for practicing. If you are trying to change a golf swing or correct a problem, swing thoughts are okay, but I believe there is a better way. This is a technique used by pros and most good golf instructors. I call them, "repetitive slow motion drills". These are drills you can do with or without a club. Most of a golf swing is about positions, where and when they occur. Ben Hogan was a strong believer in practicing a move slowly over and over again. He mentions this in his book, "Five Lessons, The Modern Fundamentals of Golf". This is a must read for the serious golfer.

For example, if you are working on takeaway, start from the setup position and move the club back to about waist high. It's called the "one piece takeaway". Simply start the swing by moving the arms and club together, not changing wrist position. Move the club back with your hands moving over the toe of your right shoe. Don't twist anything, just move the club, hands, and arms together. Your wrists may start to chock ever so slightly by waist high. This action will improve width of arc and keep your left arm straight. The toe of the clubface will point forward about 30%. This is correct. It should not point straight up. Repeat this move slowly 50-100 times. You may take a break. What you are trying to do is make this move so automatic that NO swing thought is needed. The takeaway is one of the most important parts of a golf swing. It will determine tempo, swing plane, and proper wrist angle. This will eventually be as simple as walking and you will have one less thing to think about when you play on the course with your friends. REMEMBER, the ultimate goal is to put all these practiced skills into the right brain. The left brain will no longer interfere and you will swing with ease and fluidity. No Tension.

After working on takeaway for several days, move on to the remaining portion of the backswing. Do these moves slowly and eventually at full speed. I will go into more detail later for these position moves. The point I am making is that the golf swing is really many parts. Work on learning each part by performing repetition drills and eventually you will produce a complete correct swing. I can't emphasize enough about the problem of going to the range and just swinging away at balls, using swing thoughts that may be totally incorrect, and as a result, make your golf swing worse. Don't waste time and energy at the range unless you know what you are doing.

It would be better to practice at home for a while, breaking down each part of the swing you are working on. Once you have your repetitions secure in your mind, then go to the range and work on the parts you have been rehearsing, but now using a ball. Most likely it will take some time to correct everything you have been doing incorrectly for years. If you use slow motion drills, you may reduce this time significantly. Remember, doing something repetitively will eventually become an automatic motion without thought. That is the goal.

To start, swing thoughts should only be used when practicing without a ball. Once you feel confident with some of the drills, go to the range and start hitting balls with just lofted clubs, such as 7,8,9, and PW irons. Do not swing full speed to start. Just make slower swings using some of the drills you worked on at home without a ball. You can use one swing thought at a time as long as you do not use a full speed swing.

Take your time at the range. Make 2 to 3 practice swings and then hit a ball. However, if you are working on tempo, tee up 3 or 4 balls in a row, and then step up and hit each ball one after another. Don't worry too much about setup except for the first ball. This will keep you relaxed and you will swing with a more natural swing. At the same time you can include ONE swing "feel" when making these sequential shots. Use a thought like "stay more centered when swinging". Or, "low takeaway". Or, "don't rush the start of the downswing". Or, "belt buckle to target". Or, "shake hands after impact". These are considered swing "feels". I will provide more detail for how to use these thoughts in a later chapter.

Counting is a good swing thought when working on timing. This does not inhibit the free movement controlled by the right brain. You can use for example: One, Two. "One" is the backswing, "Two" is impact. You could try One, And, Two. The "And" added for transition. Experiment with different counts to see what works best to encourage a better transition and release. Talk to your golf instructor about what works best for your swing.

Swing thoughts that are not too detailed are good to work on. Anything that is too complicated cannot be used when moving a club at <u>full speed</u>. All you will do is confuse the right brain, producing a jerky fragmented swing. I have tried some of these swing thoughts, and it sent me "down the rabbit hole". Avoid detailed swing thoughts at all costs when playing on the course. I also suggest not using on the range. These should only be used when doing slow motion drills at home, preferably in front of a mirror. The following are helpful swing thoughts, but not for full speed swings. Here is a list of detailed swing thoughts:

1. Right arm pushes out during backswing to keep left arm straight
2. Shift weight to right heel at top of backswing
3. Keep right knee more bent during backswing
4. Left knee moves toward ball during backswing
5. Left shoulder more down under chin at top of backswing
6. Keep back straighter during the swing
7. Keep left arm straighter all the way through impact
8. Keep right elbow more downward at top of backswing
9. Be careful not to cock wrists too soon during backswing
10. Pause at the top of the swing (not for everyone)
11. Speed at top of swing and transition need to be same
12. Keep left wrist flat at top of backswing
13. Be sure weight is on right heel at top of backswing
14. Keep my weight inside the right foot during backswing
15. Butt must stay more back at top of backswing
16. Hands need to drop to start downswing
17. Right elbow to side to start downswing
18. Bump left hip to target to start downswing
19. Be sure to shift weight left to start downswing

20. Right elbow moves to right pocket to start downswing
21. Right shoulder pulls right knee toward target
22. Hold wrist angle until hip high on downswing

You may have noticed that almost every one of these swing thoughts suggests the movement or position of a part of the body. As I mentioned earlier, this can be a real problem and will confuse the mind. These should not be used except when doing slow motion drills. These are the type of thoughts that can really disrupt body movements when the club is moving at 100 miles per hour. However, by using repetitive drills these swing thoughts will eventually become automatic, and then, you can swing at full speed. Full speed should not be "all out". Most good golfers swing at 80 percent of their full capacity when playing. I will discuss the details of the full swing later and you will discover that many of these swing thoughts align with the detail of the correct full swing. Swing thoughts are merely suggestions that the left brain tells the right brain how to perform. The right brain must be <u>trained</u> to perform skills at an optimal level.

What I wanted to point out in this chapter is the importance of developing a swing that is done more naturally, not overwhelmed by too many swing thoughts. The golf swing is not real complicated if it is broken down into parts. The problem for amateurs, many important parts of the swing are overlooked. All the swing thoughts I mentioned are not relevant to many golfers who are already performing many parts of the full swing correctly. If you take a few lessons, the instructor can advise you what parts of your swing require improvement or change. In conclusion, it is okay to use swing thoughts, as long as they are used with repetition practice drills. And, breaking the swing down into parts is a great way to practice. Over time, you will really improve, and your swing will feel relaxed and natural.

Chapter 2

Amateur vs. Professional

"Winning isn't everything, but wanting it is."

Arnold Palmer

"Golf is the only game I know of that actually becomes harder the longer you play it."

Bobby Jones

As an amateur, I play golf for enjoyment. But, as you know, it is a lot more fun to play golf when you hear that awesome sound of solid impact when the club makes perfect contact with the ball. You know this special sound only occurs when the ball and the "sweet" spot of the club merge at just the right time. This feel is so special that we crave to accomplish this rare occurrence every time we prepare to swing. Golf is an addiction. We often have to endure so much defeat just to obtain a fleeting moment of success. It's difficult to understand how the pros are capable of this feat of near perfect contact every time they strike the ball.

First, you have to wonder why there is such a huge difference between the swing results of the amateur vs. the professional? It is all about impact. Nothing else matters except "impact". How the ball is impacted affects spin, direction, and distance. Whatever happens before and after impact is what produced the eventual results. The amateur is rarely able to accomplish this feat since good impact can only be achieved if your body moves almost exactly the same way every time you swing the club. Just three degrees of clubface angle difference between two swings can change the landing spot of the ball by 10 yards left or right of the intended target.

During impact, amateur golfers do not compress the ball well because they have poor timing. Most golfers play only once a week or less. No one should expect to perform anywhere close to the level of a professional by playing so few times during the course of a year. Ben Hogan said he could not perform well if he missed just one day of practice. Do not add pressure to perform at a high level when you do not practice or play every day. Setting unrealistic expectations can be a major downfall for your mental state, causing you to play with too much tension, and you know what tension can do to your golf game.

Not only do professionals hit the ball further with greater accuracy, they also have a better understanding of course management. Very few amateurs have a plan before they play a round. To reduce strokes a good golfer will plan ahead for the best putting position on each green. They will study the slope of a green to determine the best approach. The pros will decide ahead of time if they want to draw or fade the ball for a better position to make a birdie. The pros know exactly how far they can hit each club in the bag. Almost ALL amateurs are short when they approach a green, always believing they will compress the ball perfectly every time. If amateurs played one extra club on each full swing approach shot on every hole, they would likely improve their score by a minimum of 5 strokes. Try it next time you play.

Pro golfers have a great short game. It takes hours and hours of practice to develop a good short game. Since the terrain of a golf course is so unpredictable every chip and pitch shot is different. Pros constantly practice hitting the ball from all types of lies. They will use different lofted clubs to control distance and how the ball will roll out or stop. This is an art form and must be practiced as much as the full swing. Unfortunately, most amateurs rarely practice chipping, which is probably the best way to save strokes. This includes sand shots, which just like chipping and pitching requires a certain technique to perform successfully. Most amateurs who have not studied the game or taken lessons would not know that there is a right and wrong way to do all these things. No different than the full swing, a lot of time is required to perfect how to swing the club in each of these cases. Chipping, pitching, and sand play can be improved with just a few lessons. I highly recommend you sign up for lessons just for these three important parts of the improvement quest. You can be an average golfer or older golfer and often score better than a fairly good golfer if you can possess a good short game. This part of the game is easy to learn and can save you 7-8 strokes or more per round. The short game also includes putting. Again there is a technique for good putting. A couple lessons here would go a long way to improve your score. When putting, you may think you are good at judging distance and speed, but do you really know how to read greens? How often do you miss putts to the right or left, and you thought you had estimated correctly. Has anyone even taught you how to read greens? There are so many facets to golf that amateurs tend to overlook.

Pros have a pre-shot routine that is the same each time they prepare to swing. A good routine will improve rhythm, concentration, and reduce tension. This is one thing amateurs should practice because it is done before the swing begins, and it requires very little time and effort. Most importantly, this will reduce tension and eliminate swing thoughts before you start taking the club back. When combined with setup, it will make the swinging of the club more fluid by following the same pattern each time. A good routine will block unwanted negative thoughts that often try to creep into your mind just before starting the backswing.

Pros seek instructional help even when they have just minor problems with their game. How many amateurs have considered lessons from an instructor when their game is going "off the rails"? If an amateur goes to YouTube to solve all their swing problems they may be going in circles. YouTube videos can work, but you must have an excellent knowledge of the golf swing, or you will often misdiagnose the real problem and get caught in a circle of changes that is never ending. If you find yourself in this situation, take a lesson from a professional instructor.

Pros have a repeatable swing. They have great fundamentals. Their setup is flawless. Every time they setup to the ball their position is the same each time, unless a different setup is needed to shape a shot. If the setup is not done properly, the entire swing has little chance of success. In the books written by Jack Nicklaus, he said that setup and takeaway were the most important parts of the golf swing. Of course, he also insisted that keeping the head in a fairly stable position through impact was just as important.

Pros have a fluid transition. Pros start their downswing at a pace that is not rushed. Bobby Jones, who was believed to have had one of the most fluid swings in golf stated that his downswing started with the same pace as his takeaway. Jack Nicklaus also said that the start of his downswing was the same speed as just before reaching the top of his backswing. Essentially, this is the same statement from two of the best golfers of all time.

Pros have a superb impact position. For every iron in the bag, the pros have forward shaft lean which is essential for good ball compression. This helps gain distance, accuracy, and control of spin. Pros have developed near perfect timing which is the only way to achieve forward shaft lean. Without proper timing the golf ball will travel little distance and your game will suffer immensely.

Pros have a graceful follow-through. The follow-through is the result of all that came before. Unless you have proper weight shift and proper turn, there will be no pose at the end of your swing. Every action that comes before produces the results of the final swing. One flaw can essentially compound itself.

Lastly, the pros possess the mental control to produce better results. A better mental approach to golf will reduce tension, create confidence and in the end lower your score. Another statement from Bobby Jones was, "in golf the most important distance is the 5 and-a-half inches between the ears".

Chapter 3

Professional Instructors/YouTube

"The more I practice the luckier I get."

Arnold Palmer

"Focus on remedies, not faults."

Jack Nicklaus

It is very important that you find a "good" golf instructor. Some golf professionals can concentrate too much on their own way of correcting a swing problem, and the swing thoughts they are suggesting just don't seem to sink in. Find a golf instructor that makes the effort to understand YOUR golf swing. Changes need to relate to your being able to implement. If you are working on transition for example, be sure that you can comprehend what swing feels the instructor is using to create the moves needed to make it happen correctly. Before you commit to a lesson, ask the potential instructor what their thoughts are about working with others concerning transition issues. The instructor must instill confidence which is half the battle. You will work harder if you believe there is a viable solution. Most good golf swings develop from hard work, proper instruction, and most importantly, what feels right for you. Most of a good golf swing is self-taught, "digging it out of the dirt", according to Ben Hogan. You will still need occasional golf instruction to keep from going "down the rabbit hole".

Since it can be expensive and there are no guarantees for finding the right instructor, it would be best to ask good golfers who they would recommend. How many lessons should you consider? I recommend taking one lesson to see if you like the instructor.

Normally, they offer package deals and if your first lesson met your expectations, they will likely offer you the opportunity to continue with the package deal, which is normally 4 or 5 lessons. Be sure to include the short game in one or two of your lessons. As I mentioned, the short game will save strokes creating more confidence, which in turn helps the full swing portion of your game. I have found from experience that every instructor has a certain skill in a specific facet of the golf swing. Try to find an instructor that is strong in the area you need the most help.

In the previous chapter I discussed YouTube as a means to obtain golf instruction. There are some really great instructors on YouTube. Using this type of instruction can be an excellent way to learn. But, as I mentioned earlier, you have to be careful not to go down the wrong path by changing something that is not the real problem. You may want to consider working with YouTube instructors that can analyze your swing. You can send them an online video and they provide feedback to correct what they see needs work.

Another means of golf instruction is to copy professional players that have swings similar to yours. You really have to consider timing and rhythm for choosing the golfer you want to copy. If you have a fast swing, choose a golfer with a faster tempo. Most of these videos are done both in full speed and slow motion. Watch the players swing over and over and hopefully their tempo and timing will give you the feel you want to attain. Some of these videos are analyzed in slow motion. One of the best ways to learn a golf swing is to practice positions in super slow motion, then gradually speed up your swing to full speed.

I wrote this book to help other golfers find an easier path to reach their goals. In the next few chapters I get into more detail on how to improve your swing with less effort. Ben Hogan was one of the greatest golfers of all time. Even to this day, no one has ever acquired a golf swing as refined as Hogan. His hard work resulted in today's modern swing with just a few exceptions. Today's swing is more upright and uses less hip turn. As the story goes, Hogan was said to take a bag of balls, and with almost any iron, hit one shot after another within a circle of just a few feet.

In conclusion, I want to address what was mentioned about golf instructors in the foreward section of the book. What must be considered when choosing an instructor is how they go about training your mind and body to complete certain moves in the golf swing. In the attempt to improve your swing you will likely be making changes that may be difficult to perform. If you have a swing fault that needs correction, you will be changing a habit you have developed over a decade or more ago. In addition to the lesson, changing your swing will require extensive practicing on your own. As I discussed in the first chapter, the correct way to make changes is to do countless repetitions of the move you want to achieve. These new moves must be done very slowly to start and without hitting a ball. If your golf instructor does not use this method of training, I suggest you look for someone that does. I can tell you from experience, it is difficult to change something you have been doing for decades. The brain must be trained to perform new motor skills. If you do not learn these skills well enough, they will not become part of your natural swing. As a result, you will be only thinking about swing thoughts when you go out on the golf course. Since the golf swing is completed in approximately one second, the mind will not be able to process any swing thoughts. The result will be confusion and tension.

Amateurs cannot think like a pro. We need more mental reinforcement to make changes. The pros know their swing so well that every part of the swing fits together like a puzzle. If they have a piece that is missing, they can put that piece into place without affecting the rest of the puzzle. If the amateur tries this, adding the one piece will scramble the remaining puzzle. Everything the amateur changes effects everything else.

The amateur must practice each part of the swing over and over so that the right side of the brain can change something it was trained to do 10 to 20 years before.

Once you find the instructor that understands your swing problems you will still need to practice on your own. Once you have rehearsed the changes and you feel confident about your progress, it is time to go to the range and start hitting golf balls. Before you were just hitting balls and only reinforcing swing faults or in some cases, adding more. The goal is to develop a more <u>natural</u> swing without swing thoughts. Be sure the instructor you choose has the same goal.

Chapter 4

Setup

"No matter how good you get, you can always get better."

Tiger Woods

"The enemy of golf is tension."

Bobby Jones

I believe that setup is the most important part of the golf swing. Other than mental preparation, and actually pulling the club out of the bag, this is where it all starts. This is the time when the adrenaline kicks in, the heart rate rises, and the brain starts thinking. Well that may be the case now, but it's time to eliminate or at least reduce these side effects.

Have you ever noticed how quickly the pros can setup to address the ball? To make a point, the quicker you can get settled comfortably over the ball, the better the opportunity to develop a fluid routine. The setup must be practiced often so that you can more accurately align yourself to the target. I have watched the pros on TV and in person, and it's amazing how perfectly they can align their feet, hips, and shoulders to the target line. And, the little time it takes them to establish their position is extraordinary. If you can setup accurately every time, you will have eliminated the main cause for not finding your target.

In golf, all that proceeds determines the outcome. Therefore, every result is based on the starting point. Setup starts when you decide which club to use. Note: Be careful not to underclub. This is the biggest mistake for all amateurs. An important part of setup is developing a routine. If you don't have a preshot routine, now is the time to start. The main reason for a routine is to do the same thing each time you prepare to swing so that it ties everything together, creating harmony, increasing focus, and reducing tension. It is the icing on the cake. When every action has a purpose there is a better chance of duplicating the same movements every time. The most important goal in golf is consistency. Most pros have a routine that could be timed within a second of being the same each time. If the pros do this, why not add a good routine to your setup. The way I see it, up until the time you start the swing, you can be as good as a pro without a lot of effort.

Since this book is about eliminating too many swing thoughts, the routine is where to stop these thoughts. Once the club is out of the bag, it's time to totally rely on all that you practiced before. The real starting point is to pull the club out of the bag thinking confidently that this shot will be the best shot you have every made. The act of removing the club from the bag should be like a switch. Flip the switch to turn on confidence and turn off negative thoughts. Leave negative thoughts and swing thoughts IN THE BAG. Every golf bag has several storage compartments. Leave one empty for placing all your negative thoughts and swing thoughts.

A routine should not be very long, maybe 20-25 seconds from start to finish. The routine starts when you line up the target behind the ball to the time the swing begins. Ideally, the routine needs to be as short as possible. This is especially important for those who have the tendency to over-think everything they do. Also, adding a rhythm to the routine is a way to improve timing and reduce tension. A typical routine would include standing behind the ball, picking a spot 2 to 3 feet in front of the ball in line with the target. Then, visualize the shot you are about to make. Next, address the ball and line up your club and body to the near target you selected. Then, look at the distant target and waggle the club 2 or 3 times. Look at the distant target again, look back to the ball, and swing. Time yourself to see how long it takes to complete the process and then practice this over and over again. After you have it "down pat", try humming a tune while doing the routine. This will help block stray thoughts. Your goal is to have rhythm as if you were doing a dance routine. I don't suggest doing this while playing. This is just to get everything in sync. I have seen some pros chew gun when playing, and I believe this is their way to maintain a rhythm and reduce stress. It has a calming effect. During the time of Hogan and Palmer they would sometimes smoke a cigarette. Chewing gum is a better option.

If for some reason there are distractions, negative thoughts, or any sense of uncertainty, back away from the ball and start your routine again. It may be necessary to make a practice swing to restart. Practice swings don't need to be part of the routine. If you take a practice swing, it is best to do it before starting your routine. Sometimes you just need to loosen up, get a feel for tempo, or you just need a restart. You will often see pros on the first tee take several swings either full, or just an easy swing. This is only to loosen up. They are not working on ANY swing thought or technique. Don't make a practice swing except to establish a feel for tempo or just to loosen muscle tension.

The next part of setup is the grip. The easiest way to establish a good grip is to align the club to the target, holding it just behind your left hip with your left arm hanging down to your side. When you hold the club mainly in your fingers and the thumb down the shaft, the left hand grip should be in an ideal position. Next, move the club directly in front of you, and then place the lifeline of the right hand over the left thumb and grip around the club with the right ring and middle fingers. The right little finger can be interlocked between the left index and middle fingers or just overlapped on top of the space between the index and middle fingers. There will be a "V" formed on each hand between the thumb and index fingers. If the "Vs" point toward the right ear, it is called a neutral grip. If the "Vs" point toward the right shoulder, it is called a strong grip. Which grip is better? Depends, the pros are split on this. If you like to fade the ball more often, then the neutral grip may be your choice. If you like to draw the ball, then the strong grip may be your choice. You can also fade or draw a shot with either grip by simply adjusting your stance relative to the ball. It is always best to consult with a professional instructor when choosing the best grip for YOU. **(See FIG. 1)**

How tightly should you hold the club? This is a confusing question and you will often get conflicting answers even from professionals. If you have strong hands, like Arnold Palmer, then thinking a lighter grip would be good. But if you have weak hands, then you will need to hold the club a little more tightly. When you setup to the ball, it is good to be relaxed, and holding the club more softly reduces tension. But once you begin the swing you will need to firm up your grip a little. Some golfers use a slight firming of the grip as a "trigger" to start their swing. This should feel natural, or you will create unwanted tension. There are other trigger methods that you may want to use. The key point is to hold the club just firm enough to maintain good control at the top of the backswing. You cannot be lackadaisical when changing directions at the top. Everyone thinks they need a graded scale from 1 to 10. Most will say 5. I would say 5 to 7 based upon your natural hand strength. The key is

GRIP

FIG. 1

The grip shown here is a neutral grip. Note the "Vs" point toward the right ear. The lifeline of the right hand sits on top of the left thumb. Also, the elbows are close together. The front of the right elbow faces more outward.

to <u>not vary pressure during</u> the swing. However, we all tighten our grip slightly at impact to absorb the force of striking the ball. This is merely instinct and does not produce tension.

Alignment is so important for making a repeatable swing. Just a few degrees of being misaligned at setup can change the landing spot for the golf ball as much as 20 to 25 yards. It can be the difference of being in the fairway or in the woods. The body and the club must be aligned to your desired target, unless you are specifically trying to shape a shot. The best way to work on alignment is to lay alignment sticks or club shafts on the ground. Place one a couple inches in front of your toes and the other parallel about 5 inches outside the ball. Both need to be in line with the target. You should use both when practicing because it emulates a train track. When standing a couple feet away from the ball, it's difficult to judge the straight line of the ball to target. By practicing with training aids, you will eventually acquire a feel by repetition. It's good to also take a club shaft and place it in front of your shoulders, hips, and knees and check if they all line up to the target. Do this often when practicing if you are not hitting your shots near the target. It is always good to go back to basics before making swing changes. Most swing problems are caused by improper setup. Any professional golfer will tell you this.

Next, how close to the ball should you stand at address? Just like grip pressure, it varies based upon the different characteristics of the player, the club being used, and the type of swing. Taller players tend to stand closer with a more upright swing while shorter players stand further away and possess a flatter swing. Heavier players also have a flatter swing. This can vary and is dependent on clubshaft length. The average golfer should hold the shorter irons with their arms hanging almost straight down from the shoulders. **(See FIG. 2)** As the club shafts get longer this distance from the body increases slightly. Only fairway woods and the driver increase a greater amount, maybe 3-4 inches further away than the shorter irons. Consult your golf instructor to be more specific. As stated earlier, golfers with flatter swings may stand a little further away from the ball.

When addressing the ball, your elbows need to be close together and relaxed. When gripping the club in front of you, the left elbow should point toward the left hip, and the right elbow toward the right hip. The inside face of the right elbow should point a little more outward than the left. This position encourages the right elbow to not "fly out" at the top of the backswing. A flying elbow will negatively affect wrist angles and improperly alter the swing path as the club moves down from the top. **(See FIG. 1)**

SETUP

FIG. 2

Setup for a lofted club. This shows how the feet, knees, hips, and shoulders are positioned in line with the target. The shoulders in this photo are slightly open to adjust for a small downhill lie. The arms are almost straight down from the shoulders, and the back is fairly straight.

Balance and stability are often not discussed much when setting up for a golf shot. This should be considered to be as important as a good grip or alignment. Without good balance, the flight of the golf ball will be unpredictable. As a golfer gets older, this may be the biggest factor, in all facets of the game, why the scores keep getting higher. Balance can affect putting and chipping as well. So how can you improve balance? Obviously, you can do yoga and weight training. But can balance be improved merely by how you setup? Good balance is mainly about how your weight is centered over your ankles. Most books and golf instructors will suggest your weight should be more centered on your feet and maybe slightly favor the balls of your feet. I have found that as I get older, I have to feel my weight more over the arches of my feet to feel stable and maintain better balance for a complete swing. This weight distribution is easily done by feeling like you are sitting on the very edge of a shorter stool. Your butt will be a little further back during setup. You can also bend your knees a little more but be careful not to get too much weight onto the heels because it will be much harder to get off the right heel to shift left in the downswing. If you are having problems with errant shots and you sense some balance issues, try adjusting your setup weight distribution just a little and you may see more consistent shots. I might add that the back must be fairly straight to facilitate a better shoulder turn. With the butt being a little more extended, the back will be naturally straighter at setup and throughout the swing.

The waggle is part of setup. It should be called a mini swing. Waggles can relieve tension, determine direction of takeaway, and establish a tempo. If you do not use a waggle, it's best to keep the club moving in some way to reduce tension. Some golfers just move the clubhead up and down behind the ball. Just choose what works and make it part of your setup routine.

At setup, the eyes must be focused on the ball, while your mind is focused on the target. Earlier I pointed out what pros do. In addition to focusing on the ball, the eyes need to remain level until impact. The way I look at it, "crooked eyes, crooked shot". Looking at the bill of your hat will tell you if you are keeping your eyes level. Level eyes will also improve balance. To prove what I am saying, turn this book or cell phone slightly sideways and try reading. It will confuse your mind and you will feel dizzy. When putting, simply looking up too soon will cause your putt to go off line. The putt is essentially following your eyes. Level eyes equals straighter shots for both putting and the full swing. Thinking eyes staying level until impact might be a solution for early extension. Give it a try and watch your score improve.

Chapter 5

Full Swing

"Every day that I missed practicing takes me one day
longer to be good."

Ben Hogan

"The road to success is always under construction."

Arnold Palmer

Everything a golfer does prior to starting the downswing will likely determine if the swing will be successful. A perfect setup routine will not produce a successful swing, but it provides a better opportunity to do so. A good golf swing is the sum of ALL the parts. Each part is dependent on what was done before. It's a building process and it requires a good foundation. The setup was the foundation, now it's time to build the rest of the structure. Starting the club back is called the takeaway. Jack Nicklaus said this was the most important part of the golf swing. This is a profound statement since, let's face it, the takeaway is the first 2 to 3 feet the club moves in the backswing. You would think "anybody can move a club two plus feet and do it perfectly". We all should be shooting par! Guess what, it is not that simple. Almost every amateur fails to do this properly. I have watched hundreds of slow motion videos of Jack Nicklaus and other golfers and I have to say, his takeaway stands out as something special. It is poetry in motion. Tiger Woods' takeaway is essentially identical. There is no way to put into words what these two great players do. You can only watch videos and try to copy what you see. So what makes the takeaway so important? Why do the greatest golfers of all time have this part of the swing so similar? The current terminology is "one-piece takeaway". One-piece stands for, everything moves together as one. Basically, you take your setup position and simply move the club, shoulders, arms, and hands back together following the arc of the outstretched left arm. By doing this, the clubface will be slightly closed and the wrists retain an uncocked position. This takeaway position will affect swing plane, wrist angles at the top of the backswing, width of arc, and determine tempo and rhythm of the entire swing. That is about all there is for completing a golf swing. Since 2 to 3 feet of movement determines so much, more time should be spent practicing takeaway than any part of the golf swing. **(See FIG. 3)**

Let's break this down in more detail. First, swing plane will relate to setup since you are moving the club away based on how bent over you are at setup. The movement of the upper body and arms during the one-piece takeaway will determine the plane of your swing. Players that stand closer at setup will have a more upright plane, where the backswing is near the right shoulder at the top of the swing. These players can produce higher loft and more downward compression on the ball. Most current pros fall into this category.

Wrist angles affect the final impact. But to have proper wrist angles at the best time, requires that the wrists evolve from start to finish. By holding onto the wrist angle at the start produces a flat left wrist angle at the top. A flat left wrist will encourage an ideal clubface

FULL SWING SEQUENCE

Takeaway   Full Turn

Transition   Shaft Lean   Extension

FIG. 3

The takeaway shows the hands, arms, shoulders, and club moving together while maintaining the grip angles. The wrists do not begin to cock until hands are outside the right hip. At the top of the swing, a full turn of the of the shoulders moves the weight to the right side. You can see the twisting of the back and hips promotes the release of energy back to the left side for impact.

angle at the top of the swing. This good wrist angle at the top almost assures a straighter clubface angle at impact. Now it is starting to become apparent how important the early part of the swing is.

When you reach out with your left arm to start the takeaway, you are beginning the wider arc that produces more power and accuracy. Think of starting the takeaway low to the ground. A wider arc encourages a straight left arm and a more repeatable swing. The one-piece takeaway and arm extension helps promote a delayed wrist cock, which also produces more power. Even though these sequences of movement are very small, they result in major consequences in the evolution of the final full swing.

Lastly, the takeaway is responsible for the tempo and rhythm (timing) of the entire swing. This is probably the most important of the four points I have presented. This is where Jack and Tiger really have something special you can't explain in words. If you watch video in slow motion for both, the takeaway cannot get any smoother. Their takeaway makes the whole swing blend together. I mentioned earlier that Bobby Jones said his transition at the top of his swing was the same speed as his takeaway. During his lifetime, all other golfers said Bobby Jones had the smoothest most effortless swing of all time. So how do you get this "smooth" takeaway and golf swing? Repetition. Repetition. Repetition.

As you continue moving the club back to waist high, you have now started to cock the wrists, but only a little. Most wrist cock is gradual, but after waist high it is a little more established. Gradually cocking the wrists is important for the evolving backswing. There is fluidity to this movement that helps extension and tempo. If this movement is rushed, your transition will be rushed. Practicing the cocking of the wrists in slow motion while completing the backswing will really help you groove a more consistent and smooth swing. Be sure not to move the hands too inside on the way back. You just continue the arc you started in the takeaway. I believe that the fluidity of the pros wrist cocking is so much better than the amateur. This is why amateurs have more issues with transition. If you watch slow motion videos of the pros, the smoothness of the wrist cocking to the top of the backswing clearly shows what the amateurs are not doing. It's what sometimes appears to be a small thing in the swing, but in reality, it is a game changer. I can't emphasize enough the importance of practicing this feel of fluidity when cocking the wrists in slow motion. You must repeat this action over and over until it feels "oily". There can be no unnatural speed changes that can destroy this smooth movement. I know the backswing occurs in less than a second, but if you rehearse the takeaway and the rest of the backswing repeatedly, you will soon feel like the rest of the swing just happens.

It is very important to understand what tempo you should use for the backswing and downswing. If your backswing is too slow, it may be the main problem you are having with timing. After you have practiced the positions for the backswing in slow motion, it's time to speed it up. Most amateurs have a slow backswing. This can often be their biggest issue for timing. If your backswing is too slow, it will most likely cause you to swing too fast to start the downswing. Remember what Bobby Jones said, "the start of the downswing should be the same speed as the takeaway. Jack Nicklaus said that "the start of the downswing is the same speed as just prior to the top of the swing". Therefore, if you are having a timing issue, speed up your backswing so you can better match up both sides of the swing. A faster backswing will likely stop the rushed downswing. Next time you are watching a PGA tournament on TV, notice how fast the pros move the club in the backswing. You will discover it is considerably faster than your current backswing. While observing them, count one-two to get the feel for the speed. You will be counting much faster than you anticipated. Try the same faster count for yourself. For pros the downswing occurs in a 3 to 1 ratio.

Pros complete the downswing to impact in roughly .22 to .25 seconds. That means their backswing is done on average in about .75 seconds. I can guarantee most amateurs will have a ratio near 4 to 1. This can definitely affect timing. So let's speed up the backswing and see what happens. I need to mention, with a quicker backswing, you will eliminate the added time you once had for swing thoughts and tension. I recently heard a pro speak after winning a major tournament say that he just concentrated on maintaining his normal quick tempo to prevent tension from creeping into his mind. He said his swing was over before he had a chance to think about the stress of the match. This can be applied to the setup routine. If you have a shorter routine, the chances of negative thoughts getting into your head will be greatly reduced or eliminated. Again, it's like swinging a bat to hit a baseball. The ball is moving so fast you have little chance to think. You merely react to the sudden approach of the ball. One important point, you cannot rush a golf routine and swing to the point whereas all the basics are lost. The basics of setup, takeaway, and specific positions are required to produce a good swing. <u>You must have time to complete the backswing</u>. You just need to find the right speed that works for you. A slow swing is good for wedge play and chipping. It is important to base the speed of your backswing on your ability to maintain a similar speed to start the downswing. Tempo is more about a pace that feels comfortable based upon your personality. Never feel like you are rushing a golf swing.

As you near the top of the backswing, the wrists become almost fully cocked with the club and left arm near an angle of 90 degrees. The left arm MUST remain as straight as possible at the top of the swing. Most amateurs have a problem keeping the left arm straight because they are trying to increase the length of their backswing. This is a real problem for many reasons. First, it immediately creates inconsistency affecting the swing path and grip. Secondly, it reduces the coiling of the body which greatly decreases swing speed. Thirdly, it will change tempo and produce an early release of the clubhead, causing the flipping of the club at impact. This will eliminate forward shaft lean, which is necessary for good compression of the ball. These are really significant issues. Amateurs should spend a lot of time practicing keeping their left arm straight throughout the swing. During the backswing the right arm can push out more to help promote a straight left arm. **(See FIG. 4)** Keeping the left arm straight may feel forced at first, but after making MANY slow motion backswings, the extension will feel more natural. I don't like the suggestion that the arms be very relaxed during the golf swing. The arms must be in control of the club. The sense of firmness is the arms should be the same as the grip pressure, a feel of

RIGHT ARM EXTENSION

FIG. 4

In order to increase the width of arc, the right arm can push out as you move the club in the backswing. In addition, this helps maintain a straight left arm. A straighter left arm and wider arc will increase your distance.

being in control, not soft. A straight left arm must start with the takeaway. The feel of starting the takeaway lower to the ground, with the sense you are pushing a ball along the ground will help promote a wider arc.

Transition is probably the one segment of the golf swing, wherein there exists the greatest difference between the pro and amateur. Transition begins at the top of the backswing and ends at the start of the release of the club for impact. Since the downswing to impact is typically near one fourth of a second, the transition occurs in the "blink of an eye". Yet, it is transition that will literally make or break the golf swing. The worst enemy for a good transition is tension in the wrong places, specifically the hands, arms, and shoulders. However, there will be tension in the back, hips, butt and legs. At the top of the swing these parts have coiled like a spring so the energy can be released in the downswing. So, if someone tells you that you must be relaxed in golf to produce an ideal swing, they are somewhat mistaken.

So what actually occurs during transition? Once the top of the backswing is reached and the body has fully coiled, there is no option but for the body to reverse direction and return to a position not too different than it was at the start of the swing. Basically, what goes up, must come down! Transition is all about gravity and stored energy and how to use it optimally. So, we first need to understand the physics behind the transition move before we can create the action of the golf swing. Too often, we get in the way of what the body and gravity do naturally. If you over-think the transition move, you will NEVER allow your natural ability to do what is necessary for success.

Gravity is the force that keeps our feet planted to the ground. Gravity will pull the weight of the arms and club towards the ground without our muscles doing anything. So if you want to add speed to your golf swing you must use gravity in the best way possible, and not let our muscles take away what is ordinary physics. Gravity and muscles must work together properly to initiate a good transition. You have often heard the phrase in golf "staying centered". This is suggesting how we work with gravity. When we move our bodies from place to place we are using our sense of balance and gravity in harmony. As humans, we learned to walk using this harmony. In martial arts the center of gravity for our body is located about 4 inches below the navel. This is called the "dan-tien". Some players may refer to this center point as their "core". When we swing a golf club we often think about the belt buckle pointed towards the ball as we near impact, and facing the target as we complete the follow-through. Now you can see the significance of these thoughts. It is our way of combining the balance of martial arts and the golf swing. All golfers should develop more mental focus with regards to our center of gravity. Good balance is the foundation of a natural golf swing. When your golf swing is failing, don't always change something. Instead, go back to basics and concentrate on what is happening with your center of gravity (dan-tien). If you are more aware of your "dan-tien" during the backswing and transition, you will be able to perform the golf swing with the balance and fluidity that you are striving for. So gravity is what we need to use to our advantage. There is a specific time when gravity can be felt the most, and that is the time when the golfer switches direction at the top of the swing. If done correctly, the weight of the club should be sensed at the top of the swing. As the body starts to press into the ground to start the downswing, the weight of the clubhead is resisting the change in direction as the body starts to unwind. The clubhead is almost floating in space as the hands are pulled on by the uncoiling body. What is happening, the weight of the clubhead is lagging behind as the hands and arms wait to be pulled around by the lower body that is pushing forward into the ground. The force of inertia from the backswing is creating this feel. Jack Nicklaus said in his book, "Golf My Way" that his being able to sense the weight of the club at the top of the swing contributed greatly for performing the transition move with such fluidity. When you practice, try to sense the weight of the club at the top of our swing, and the transition should be accomplished with greater success.

The body coils like a spring when you move your body around during the backswing. The spring is torqued until it eventually reaches a point where it must release the energy to spring back. The spring is attached to the ground by your feet. Energy is released from the ground up as the body uncoils. If you turned your hips and shoulders properly, the body will spring back based on the tension you created by the twisting motion. The greater the tension, the faster the body wants to spring back. This is why it is important to complete the backswing. Cutting it short or bending your left arm will destroy this coiling tension and greatly reduce the spring back action.

Once the club and hands reach the top of the backswing, there is a lateral forward shift of the hips and knees because the body wants to return to its original starting point. The body seeks to return to its "dan-tien". Since the lower body moves first, the upper body hesitates for a split second to start to unwind. This is what some call a pause. This is when the hands and club pause to change direction. Depending on how quick you shift the body left will determine the amount of pause. For most golfers, this is such a small amount of time and the pause is not obvious. But for others, with a slower transition tempo, the pause is more apparent. The shift left must be the first move before starting down, and it must be smooth. If the shift is late or jerky, the entire swing will be out of sequence and the arms and hands will move first producing an "over-the-top" downswing. If you let the force of gravity do its job, the transition will be an easier process. When the shift is done properly, the hands, arms, and clubhead will feel almost weightless before the left hand/arm pull down on the clubhead. Also, when the shift to the left occurs first, the club handle will drop down from its original arc and place the club handle in an ideal plane for releasing it through the impact zone. When playing shorter or more lofted clubs, and of course you are closer to the ball, you should feel like your upper left arm pushes off the left peck as you change direction. What happens, is, the body starts to unwind while the left arm and club are still moving back to finish the backswing. This creates the pressure between the peck and upper left arm. This sensation will feel like a springboard for the start of the downswing. It can also produce more power.

Also critical for a good transition, the shoulders must rotate around the spine along the same plane. The spine angle must be maintained during the swing, or the swing will fail. Most amateurs have a poor shoulder turn. They have a tendency to be too flat, with the left shoulder not staying down and below the chin at the top of the backswing. Poor shoulder rotation will affect swing plane, which will in turn affect the transition move. Do not raise your upper body as you rotate around on the backswing.

The right knee position during the backswing will also affect transition. The right leg and knee are the anchors for the backswing. It is the stabilizing pivot point for the coiling of the spring. If this anchor is not secure, the tension of the spring is lost. Without this lock to the ground, the turn of the body will be a waste of time. If the right knee straightens more than just a small amount during the backswing, most of the spring tension of the body will be lost. The right knee should remain flexed and pointed slightly forward during the backswing. This stable right leg must not let the weight of the body move to the outer part of the foot. **(See FIG. 5)** The weight must remain on the inside of the right foot preventing the lower body from swaying to the right. It is almost impossible to hit an accurate shot when the body sways right and then has to return back to center for impact. The body must remain more centered for consistency. Once the body's center point has moved during the swing, maintaining balance is very difficult. Retaining a bent right knee will promote more weight shift to the right heel and butt. When you get more weight into the glutes,

FIG. 5

The top of this backswing is in the ideal position. First, the right knee has remained bent and firm to anchor her coiled body. The position of the left arm is just above the right shoulder. The left wrist is flat and matches the alignment of the clubface. You can see her weight has shifted to the right heel and glute area. This becomes a springboard to move weight forward.

you can generate more muscle stretch that will provide the ability to jump and throw your lower body into the swing. This allows you to use ground force to gain distance. A good example is Rory McIlroy, who uses more ground force and glute muscles to increase clubhead speed. During transition he squats down just a split second as he starts down from the top of the swing, and then pushes off his right side to rotate around and through the swing. This is called the squat move, originally used by Sam Snead in the 40s and 50s. This move relies on a bent right knee and a good weight shift. Even if you have a problem trying the squat move, it is still important to use the pressure into the right glute for generating better speed and timing.

The last part of the transition is timing. I discussed this some already, but a few summary points. You can make a lot of mistakes in a golf swing and still hit the ball well if you have great timing. You may have consistency issues but, you may still make good contact. Good timing in golf is the ability to smoothly sequence from one move to the next. All good timing relies on good setup, smooth takeaway and well-timed weight shift during transition. Good timing is easier if your hands move at the same speed just before and just after the top of the swing. You cannot rush the hands until the lower body has shifted left.

Chapter 6

Impact

"You must play boldly to win."

Arnold Palmer

"The object of golf is to beat someone. Make sure that someone is not yourself."

Bobby Jones

It's the moment of truth. No turning back. Every move that has gone before will now come to light. Will impact be a success or failure? What is fact, it is not coincidence that every professional golfer enters the impact zone in almost identical fashion. So what needs to be done to duplicate this pattern of success. Good impact is dependent on specific positions during setup, backswing, and transition. Even though pros may differ slightly proceeding impact, they always reach the point of release with the club just below waist high, and the shaft pointing towards the target. The wrists and clubface are parallel to the target. The wrists have remained cocked and the hands are positioned near the right thigh. Balance, just before impact, is the key to success of the square solid strike. If you can discover the correct tempo for your personality then you will create the harmony needed for good balance. It is so important to work on tempo and timing until you are "blue in the face". Near perfect timing will bring all positions in the golf swing together at the right time. Spend time at the range working solely on tempo and timing, the two "Ts". I must emphasize again the importance of the takeaway for good timing. You need to practice different takeaway speeds to see what works best. A faster takeaway may be all you need to improve timing. As I mentioned earlier, the pros swing with a 3 to 1 ratio. The swing to impact is just 1 second. If you can get close to their swing tempo you will definitely be a better golfer. I have rarely seen golfers at the range using a fast tempo. Amateurs always want to be in control, believing that you have to start with a slow backswing. This is a big mistake. If you do not have any momentum (energy) from the start of the swing it is harder to do it from the top without tightening your grip and rushing the swing. This is a major point. If you have the correct tempo it is less likely you will rush the downswing. Do not rush, just slightly increase your backswing speed and the rest of the swing will take care of itself.

Be sure to not release the wrist cock you had at the top of the swing too soon. As the right hand is poised for release, it will be in the position as if you were shaking hands with someone next to your right side. As your hands move through impact the right hand reaches out to shake hands with someone standing beside you in the direction of the target. You should feel like you have to stretch to reach for the handshake. All the while your head will remain down and near the back of the ball line. The position of the head through impact is critical. By keeping the head in position, the movement of the club will remain on plane, as the shoulders rotate around the spine. If the head moves forward too soon, your hands and club will fall behind and create an open clubface, producing a slice. If the head pops up too soon, the shoulders will move up creating a different arc and the hands will flip the club through impact for an early release. Some may title this move, "early extension". This will normally cause the clubface to close, producing a hook. If you watch professional golfers closely you can see how their head stays in position through impact. Some pros drop their head, but what is really happening if you look more closely, the base of the neck has not moved. This is where the shoulders turn, not around the head. If the head remains fairly close to the same position from the start of the swing until just past impact, normally the shot will be fairly straight. Also, the shoulders and hips will be in a good position throughout the swing. This is a difficult part of the swing that must be practiced. There is a fine line for maintaining the position of the head verses being too still. If the head is frozen in place the body will not be able to turn properly. The head has to move slightly to prevent injury to the neck or back. Remember, tension in the neck and shoulders is not good for a more relaxed swing. I prefer using a swing thought that does not involve "keep my head still". Avoid any swing thoughts that can produce tension. Using the bill of your hat by visually keeping it centered above the ball throughout the swing will keep your head level, and prevent you from raising up too soon. This may be the <u>best solution for eliminating early extension</u>. I know I said no swing thoughts while playing.

This swing thought is okay to use on the course because it is just about staying focused. It is so important to maintain head position until after impact.

Tempo and keeping the head fairly stable should be rehearsed every time you go to the range. If both of these facets of the game are done well, your impact will improve greatly. The movement of the wrists through the impact zone needs to be automatic because it happens so fast, likely less than a tenth of a second. Practice the handshake drill and it will also improve impact.

Impact should include some forward shaft lean. This position can only occur when your timing and tempo are in sync. The best method for developing forward shaft lean is by hitting long low pitch shots. You will need to hold off the follow-through for this type of shot. This shot encourages keeping the hands ahead of the clubhead. When you practice, take the club back to just above waist high and finish the follow-through at about chest high and hold the finish. Do this over and over until you feel like you have the forward shaft lean you want. Tour average for irons is just over 10 degrees of lean at contact. Also, be careful not to lift the head too soon. Keep the head down and slightly behind the ball. Keep your eyes level until impact. Practice with a slower tempo swing, and then gradually speed it up while increasing the backswing and follow-through.

Chapter 7

Follow-Through

"If you can't outplay them, outwork them."

Ben Hogan

"A golfer has to train his swing on the practice tee, then trust it on the course."

Bob Rotella

When you attend a PGA tournament, you can personally witness the grace and poise of the tour player as they finish each shot. You could compare their follow-through and pose to that of a ballet dancer. Their balance at the finish of the swing is absolutely astonishing. The pose at the end of the swing can only happen if the entire swing is done with upmost precision. How can you copy this great finish? It is the result of thousands of hours of hard work and training. Obviously, the average golfer will not have this ability to practice incessantly. To finish with a "pose" as the pros do, requires near perfect balance during the shifting of weight from the right side to the left side. To finish with about 90% of your weight on the left foot and 10% on your right toe is an accomplishment that can appear surreal. I cannot recall playing with any amateurs that have a 10 handicap or higher that have this type of "pose" finish. Normally, if you cannot finish in a balanced fashion, most likely, some part of the swing needs to be corrected.

The shifting of weight from right to left is where your balance will likely get off track. I always return to the concept of knowing where your dan-tien is, as you move through the entire swing. I have found that the first move of the takeaway is where balance problems start. When doing the takeaway you should feel the rotation of your upper body moving around the area of the dan-tien.

This is so important to great balance. If you do not rotate around this center core, your swing will be off balance from the start. Try rotating your shoulders back and forth and feel the area about 4 inches below you belly button, as your rotation point. It is a special feel that is so important to the golf swing. This is where you can come close to perfect rotation and promotes great balance. If you don't feel this sensation of rotation around this core, you are not doing it correctly. Keep trying this until it feels like everything is in balance around this center point. It is one of the most important components of starting a golf swing. If you start right, you often end right.

Basically what the golfer needs to do is think of the golf swing as a dance move. Your feet must be the part of the body that works with the upper body to create better balance. You must use the ground properly to have good balance. Your feet are your only connection to the ground, so this is where it all starts by sensing the ground to provide stability. If you can establish a mental connection to your feet it will help you establish the feeling of a firm foundation. I am dwelling on this point about balance because it is essential to creating a good finish.

There are certain elements that must be considered for a good follow-through. I spoke about the right arm extension after impact. Using the resemblance of shaking hands with someone in front of you is an ideal analogy. This is a good move because by the time the right arm is waist high in front of you, the hands need to be in a thumbs-up position. **(See FIG. 6)** Your head has been staying focused on the ball area until your right shoulder begins to push it around. Following the extension of the arms at waist high, the upper body and hips are pulled around by the force of the swing until they face the target. This is where you use the swing thought of "belt buckle to target". With the belt buckle facing the target the momentum of your arms and golf club will continue to pull your upper body around.

The pose should have the left arm bent at 90+ degrees to your side with the shoulders turned about 30 to 40 degrees past the hip line. I have seen many pros with their right shoulder turned so far that it points to the target. The club should come to rest over your left shoulder and behind your head. The right knee should touch or nearly touch the back of the left knee. Practice these positions over and over until they become engrained into your swing. Even though you may mishit a shot now and then, at least your finish should impress your fellow golfers.

(See FIG. 7)

FOLLOW-THROUGH EXTENSION

FIG. 6

This illustrates the moment after impact which shows the full reach in the follow-through. You can see how her hands have turned through impact creating the appearance of the right hand reaching to shake hands with someone in front of her.

FOLLOW-THROUGH FINISH

FIG. 7

If your swing is near perfect, this position will be the result. The club handle behind your head, belt buckle facing the target, and the knees touching. Practice this pose as often as possible, then finish this way every time you make a full swing.

Chapter 8

Chipping

"The only way to win tournaments is with the short game."

Phil Mickelson

"I smile at obstacles."

Tiger Woods

You're watching a major golf championship on TV. It's a Sunday final round and you are witnessing the top players in the world go head-to-head in their effort to make history. The professional golfers are all playing at near the same level of greatness. It's a close match. The players are all driving the ball far down the fairway and their wedge shots are near perfection. But, when the players reach the most difficult holes on the course, near the end of the match, suddenly the leaders' approach shots are missing the green. This is where the most memorable shots of the tournament determine the eventual winner. What is it that you remember most, when all is said and done? It is a chip-in from 15 yards off the green. The player celebrates with a fist pump or throws the club in the air. This may have been the winning shot. The short game is what separates the excellence of these great players. If you look back into golf history, you will find that most championships were won by the players who possessed the best short game, not the ones who drove the ball over 300 yards. It is often a chip or putt that determined the winner. I start this chapter by suggesting that if you want to improve your score, the short game is what really makes the difference. How many times have you played golf with someone who had a crazy swing and rarely found the green in regulation, but for some reason, that player always ended the round with the best score. When you thought about it later, you recall they were chipping the ball close to the pin on nearly every hole. Then, you finally realize it is time to dedicate more time to this part of the game.

The best part about improving the short game, practice can be done in your backyard. The short game includes 4 sectors of the game: chipping, pitching, bunker play, and putting. In this chapter, we will be discussing chipping and pitching. What is the difference? A chip shot is a shorter shot and is where the ball rolls more than it flies in the air. The pitch shot is one where the ball flies in the air more than it rolls. A pitch shot is normally a longer shot – typically 25 to 50 yards.

Just like the full swing, a chip shot can be performed with more consistency and accuracy if you follow a specific setup and swing technique. As in all sports and in golf, there are players that use different or unusual methods to accomplish similar results. A few players have been very successful using methods not normally taught by professional golf instructors. Nothing against these different methods, but if you are looking for consistency, there is a reason 90 percent of professional golfers have a very similar setup and swing technique. This is because these tried and true methods have proven successful for the best players over time.

Many amateurs also have mental issues when facing challenging shots. Most of this stems from the fact that amateurs play less than 2 times a week. Since you are not placing the ball on a tee, every chip shot has a different challenge. Sometimes the ball may be on a tight lie with so little grass, whereupon the ball must be struck with near perfect contact to avoid sculling or chunking. Since pros play often, they have seen nearly every possible lie. I have to say, chipping and pitching is 75% confidence, and 25% technique. If you stand over a difficult shot with ANY negative thoughts, there is a 100% chance it will be a poor shot. This can sometimes happen to the best players. I have discovered, after having the "yips" at one point in my golfing life, confidence is only possible with 100% commitment. I cannot overemphasize the importance of commitment. The same can be said for putting, but with chipping the challenge of the different lies changes everything. When I developed the "yips", the only way I could escape this problem was to practice with my eyes closed. I hit many good shots with my eyes closed. It is amazing how often you can strike the ball accurately without looking. And, even if I mishit the ball, it was never that bad of shot. When you close your eyes, establishing distance is quite accurate because you swing with amazing feel. Now I play with my eyes open (no more yips), and I can credit practicing with my eyes closed to solve the problem.

With your eyes closed, all you visualize is a picture in your mind of the target, and you swing accordingly. There are no distractions. This is why visualizing the shot is so important. A good chipper needs to first visualize the shot with your eyes open or even closed, and then swing (eyes open, of course). I recommend practicing chip and pitch shots with your eyes closed to gain confidence and to improve your visualization techniques.

Let's first look at the setup recommended by instructors. The goal is to strike the ball consistently, avoiding sculls and chunks. When hitting a 100 yard wedge shot, you will be hitting more downward into the ball and creating a divot in front of the ball. This will create more spin on the ball. When chipping we desire to strike the ball to create just a little loft and then roll towards the hole. The swing must have a wider arc for this to take place. To accomplish this, the shoulders must be more level. Granted, the right shoulder will always be a little lower because the right hand is below the left on the grip of the club. So you have to adjust your upper and lower body to compensate for this. By loading more weight on the left side, bending the left knee a little more, and leaning the upper body slightly left, your shoulders will be close to level. The center of the upper body needs to line up slightly ahead of the ball. As I said before, your goal is to create a flatter wider arc when striking the ball.

By setting up this way it almost eliminates mishits. There are additional things required to make the swing more reliable. With the center of the body slightly ahead of the ball, the bottom of the arc of the swing will be slightly ahead of the ball. Also important, the head must not move up or down or side to side. Before, in the full swing you should not use the swing thought, "keep your head still". For chipping you need to practice with this thought in mind. Chip shots are performed at a slower clubhead speed, therefore you need to contact the ball very precisely. Any slight change in the upper body height, or if it sways back and forth, will normally produce a mishit.

Before discussing the swing moves, it is also important to know where and how to stand relative to the ball. To be more accurate and have more feel when chipping, it is best to stand closer to the ball at setup. It is good to stand no further than 12 inches away. Closer is okay. This means you will stand taller. Do not bend over like putting. Also, grip down on the club, just a couple inches above the bare shaft. Choke down more for longer clubs. Standing closer brings the club straighter back when swinging, which improves consistency. Remember, chipping is a lot like putting. Often the ball may be just off the green. Many good golfers will use a putting grip, and then swing a less lofted iron as if they had a putter in hand.

The feet should be close together when chipping. As close as a couple inches for short chips and 4 to 5 inches when chipping from over 15 yards off the green. The narrow stance helps your body stay centered and turn through the shot. The stance should be slightly open, again to help take the club back straighter, and encourage a better follow-through. The ball position is also important. With you feet close together the ball should be positioned just inside the back foot. This is close to center since your feet are close together. If you want a little more loft, the ball can be a little more forward as long as the hands are still in front of the ball at setup.

When gripping the club, it is best to use a weaker grip since you are close to the ball and standing taller. Weaker meaning turning your hands more left on the grip of the club. Your left thumb may be near center down the grip. Also, your hands on the club should be aligned forward 2 inches in front of the ball (forward shaft lean). If you need more loft for your shot, do not have the club shaft less than straight. The key is to NEVER let the clubhead get ahead of your hands at setup or during the swing.

Now, let's look at the swing. Chipping is much easier if you use very little hinge with the wrists. Some instructors may say no wrist hinge, which is good for real short chips. Too avoid being rigid and to reduce tension, it is best to let the wrists hinge slightly in the backswing. If you are performing a pitch shot then you will use more wrist hinge. I will discuss the pitch shot later. When moving the club back, the shoulders do most of the work, similar to a longer putting stroke. The club moves only a little inside, on its path away from the ball. Because this is a shoulder rotation swing, there will be only a little movement of the knees. The knees are not frozen but only rock a small amount during the swing. This rocking motion will provide better feel for the shot. There must be a relaxed feel for this swing, since you are not being aggressive with the swing. The arms and shoulders must be relaxed similar to putting. You still must maintain a muscle control as you do in putting. The grip pressure cannot be too light. If you have a clean lie the grip may be lighter, but if the ball is positioned in deep grass, you have a firmer grip to maintain control. In other words, the harder your swing the firmer the grip but this must be only a slight change in pressure. You do not want tension.

Taking the club back may be slow, but coming down to the ball must be slightly faster. If done correctly, it will feel like there is a mini pause at the back of the swing. This feel happens because the swing is slow not rushed. If you are jerky at all, there will be no feel in the shot. The pace of the backswing should change only a very small amount for different distances. The only time the pace may be more energetic is when there is a thick lie and then you use a short and faster backswing to promote a more aggressive move to the ball that needs to travel a short distance. This is always a tricky shot and must be practiced to attain the right feel. It is the amount of backswing that normally determines the distance you want the ball to travel.

The head is the fulcrum for a good chip shot. If you move your head, you will not be able to contact the ball consistently. In addition to the head not moving the left arm must remain straight, but not stiff, during the swing. Since the swing is slower, you must reduce the chance for error. The distance from the left shoulder to the bottom of the clubhead cannot change if you intend to strike the back of the ball in the correct spot. A good swing thought for practice is to imagine the ball is sitting on a tee, pressed almost flush to the ground, and swing with the feel you are clipping the top of the tee. The ball just gets in the way of the swing. This thought works great for tight lies. This helps overcome negative thoughts that might arise when the ball must be struck more precisely. This thought takes your focus away from the ball. If you focus on the ball for a tight lie, I can guarantee, the shot will be doomed to failure. The target must be the tee or where you are aiming. This is one swing thought that may be used when playing because it is target oriented. It is important that your target cannot be the ball. If your focus is misplaced with the ball being the target, you will only experience stray feelings of uncertainty, which produces tension. As a result, there is absolutely NO chance for success. I have experienced this myself, both with the focus on the ball and failure, and later focus on a target and success. You can practice this targeted focus and change your game.

If you are having an issue with what pace to swing, I strongly encourage you to count for timing when swinging. You can use, one, two. Take the club back on one, and strike the ball on two. On the Golf Channel, Martin Hall, said to use 1,2,1. Back on one, two, then one coming back to the ball. This encourages a quicker downswing. You never want to slow down coming back to the ball. This works great on the course as well. You can change the pace of the count to control distance. I try to avoid swing thoughts on the course, but using 1,2,1 count for chipping has made a major difference for me on the course. It is one of the best swing thoughts I have found to improve the chipping game and it does not interfere with the freedom your right brain requires for a good swing. I would call this a "swing feel". As I mentioned previously, swing FEELS can sometimes be used on the course, but you must discover which ones work for you. And, you must not use more than one swing feel while playing on the course.

When you follow-through on a chip shot, your arm and wrist structure should be maintained. The follow-through is short because your backswing was short. However, the follow-through should always be a little greater than the backswing because the speed coming down to the ball is greater. Hold the end of the swing with your hands still AHEAD of the clubhead, and I can guarantee, you will have a better strike. You could say, "the better the pose, the better the shot". **(See FIG. 8)**

What club do you use for chipping? It could be almost any club. More often, it is the less lofted clubs, i.e., 6, 7, or 8 irons. Some will use 9 or PW, depending on the lie. Since you are trying to make the ball run out to the hole, the lower lofted clubs are normally used. The lower lofted clubs are easier to use because there is less chance of mishitting the ball. The lower the loft, the more the club behaves like a putter. Pick a spot where you want the ball to land and how much you want the ball to roll, then choose the club that is more likely to complete the task. If you feel uncertain and nervous with a difficult

CHIPPING FINISH

FIG. 8

When completing the chipping stroke, the hands must finish ahead of the clubhead. This guarantees a solid strike and online finish. Notice how this player maintains head position throughout the swing. The arms, hands, and shoulders are in a perfect finish position.

shot, choose a club with less loft, like a 6 or 7 iron, and swing with confidence. Some golfers have a favorite club, and use it most of the time. This is okay, because confidence always outweighs correctness. However, it is best to be flexible because specific clubs are better to attain the best results.

With more level terrain, many golfers will use a 7 iron even when they are 50 yards away from the pin. Although the ball may fly 20 yards, then bounce, and roll 30 yards, this is not a chip, instead, it is called a pitch and run. The pitch shot normally involves the ball having more flight and less roll. There are many circumstances that determine what type of shot is required. Let's say, your ball sits 15 yards from the green and there is a sand trap in between. You will need to fly the ball over the sand trap, land on the green, and run to the hole. You would pick a lofted club, such as a lob wedge, to perform this feat. This would be called a pitch shot. If you were 75 yards away with the same circumstances, this would be considered an approach shot or generically called a wedge shot. Most pitch shots are within 25 to 50 yards from the pin. There is no definitive term based on distance. It's okay to call a 75 yard shot a pitch shot. The word "pitch" should not be used for full swing shots.

The pitch shot is very similar to the full swing except that it is a shorter and slower swing. The setup for the pitch shot is what I call a "softer" version of the full swing. Everything is closer. The feet are closer together, the ball is closer, and the upper body is more bent over. The muscles are more relaxed, since there is much less twist and turn. The grip is softer, since there is little strength involved to produce an easy flowing swing. The stance is more open, and your weight favors the left side.

The backswing is much shorter, the hands never getting above chest high. The pace is much like a long chip shot and again the distance is dependent on the amount of backswing. The pitch shot involves the use of wrists and body just like a mini full swing. One difference is the backswing requires an earlier cocking of the wrists. The shorter the pitch shot, the sooner the wrists must be cocked. For a shorter pitch shots, the wrists may only cock half way or even less. The shorter pitches require some upper and lower body rotation, but it should feel like a ¼ to ½ swing, depending on distance.

Many techniques used for the chip shot are applicable to the pitch shot, especially those inside 30 yards. This would include counting for rhythm/tempo, keeping your head almost stationary, focus on landing areas, straight left arm, keeping hands ahead of the clubhead, determining distance, and holding the follow-through.

The main difference between pitching and the full swing is the feel for distance. The only way to develop the feel for how to swing is to practice how far the ball will travel, based on tempo and the amount of backswing. Since you are close to the pin, the aim is normally of less concern. So all you need to work on is distance control. The type of lie may also affect how far the ball may travel, so a lot of practice is required to master distance control.

Chapter 9

Putting

"I don't fear death, but I sure don't like those three-footers for par."

Chi Chi Rodrigues

"A routine is not a routine, if you have to think about it."

Davis Love Jr.

Few books on golf discuss putting. Not sure why, considering that every tournament I have ever watched on TV, the winner was determined by the golfer who made a challenging putt near the end of the match. You would think that there should be a significant number of books on this subject. I have read that Ben Hogan did not like putting. At one point, he expressed how the game would be better without it. The average golfer rarely talks about putting. Media and golf analysts discussions normally center around topics other than putting. You might conclude there is less glamour and excitement when it comes to the topic of putting. Yet, most winners are determined by who makes the critical putts when everything is on the line.

It's difficult to teach someone how to putt. It is such a personal matter. Everyone has a particular style of putting that is only good for them. I have never seen any two players that putt in an identical fashion. Yet, why do some players appear to make a large percentage of their putts, while others miss almost every putt they attempt. Even though some amateurs are good putters, they are rarely good at making longer putts. So, you have to think, there must be some missing links that are required for being a great putter. This chapter is about finding the missing links that are common to the greatest putters.

I have played with an untold number of golfers, and for some reason I have never seen two players use the same putter. It is as though there are as many putters as there are golfers! This also applies to putting styles. Everyone grips and swings their putter differently. The pros are no exception. In conclusion, you have to wonder, is there a standard for putting? Obviously the answer is "No". But, just like chipping, certain basics apply that can improve the possibility of seeing the ball go into the cup more often.

I will start with equipment. Some putters are better than others. I will not mention brand names, but once you've picked up and swung the normally more expensive putters, you discover they seem to have better balance. They want to swing themselves. At first, this special feel is very apparent, but you later discover that it is the one holding the club that matters most. After you swing other putters you are not so convinced the expensive putter is for you. We are all so different when deciding what putter is best. It is so difficult to tell the difference after swinging 10 different putters. It's a little like wine tasting. After a while they all start tasting the same. Once you find the right "feel", that's it. When you decide on the putter, it is not about price. You need a putter that gives you confidence. Purchasing a well balanced putter is still better, as long as it feels right for you. A golf professional can also provide some assistance for deciding which putter to purchase.

Some of the new larger putter grips that are now available can make a big difference in how you hold the club. The larger grips provide more feel. This is because you can hold the club with a lighter grip pressure and still have the same stability you had with some smaller grips. Lighter grip pressure equals better feel. Most of the large grips are square, which helps maintain alignment. The larger grip provides more room for the thumbs to be positioned on the top of the square grip. The thumbs are so important for the feel and consistency of the swing. Most of the pros are now using the larger grips.

Does how you grip the putter affect consistency? Yes and No. Yes, if you are a novice or you're having major issues. No, if you have been using the same grip for some time and you are making a good percentage of your putts. In other words, "if it ain't broke, don't fix it". There are ways, however, that can improve your grip for better results. The most important way to improve feel is to be sure you position both thumbs on the top of the putter grip. This will also improve stability for moving the putter back and forth. The position of the thumbs will help combine the hands. Also, the hands can be tied together by overlapping the fingers. The goal is for the two hands to become a unit. If one over powers the other, the swing will be off-line. It is okay to have a dominant hand but the two hands must still work in harmony. This is more of a feel issue. If you want to feel as though the right hand is pushing the left hand through the swing, that will be fine as long as the two hands maintain even pressure on the grip handle. The right hand dominance is a "feel", not a stronger grip that guides and pushes the club. The hands must be a unit and not battle for control. Many of the pros have changed to a grip called "left hand low". Just like it sounds, the left hand is lower on the grip, instead of the standard that most have used since the beginning of golf. **(See FIG. 9)** I used this standard grip until about 10 years ago, when for some reason, out the blue, I got the yips. It was the same time I got the yips when chipping. The yips are the result of being nervous and becoming uncertain about how you want to move your arms and hands to make the club hit the ball properly. It is normally the result of over-thinking something and you let uncertainty be the controlling force. The brain basically short circuits and causes the muscles in your arms and hands to suddenly tighten producing a flinch or jerk. A simple way to describe the cause is, the left part of your brain is fighting for control with the right part of the brain and neither one wins. I decided to experiment with the "left hand low" grip. This solved my problem. I cannot explain, but it worked for me. It did take a while to adapt. But, after adjusting my

LEFT HAND LOW

FIG. 9

This photo shows the hands on the putter with the left hand below the right, "Left hand low". The thumbs of both hands are positioned on top and aligned comfortably down the shaft. This grip drops the left shoulder to help move the club with a better pendulum motion.

hands and fingers into different overlapping positions, I found a comfortable grip, and no more yips. If your putting is very inconsistent or you develop the yips, give this style of grip a try. With the left hand lower it encouraged better shoulder rotation. This occurs because the left hand lower makes the shoulders more level at setup and during the swing. It also keeps the wrists stable, and my hands were more unified. Both hands feel more connected to the arms and shoulders, which encourages a better pendulum style of movement.

There are many types of grips. Whatever grip you chose, it must meet certain objectives. First, you must feel that the hands and club are unified. There must be no wobble when you move the club back and forth. The hands, arms, and club must move smoothly together. Secondly, each hand must have even pressure on the grip of the club. If one hand is dominant, it could cause the club to be flipped through impact. The result is an off line strike. Thirdly, the grip must be repeatable. The hands need to be positioned on the club the same way every time. Lastly, the grip must help maintain wrist stability and at the same time be tension free.

Is there a recommended procedure for how to stand and address the ball? It is preferable that your body align the same every time you address the ball. Once you choose the line for the ball to travel, your body should be in parallel alignment with the aim line. This would include feet, hips and shoulders. This is preferred. A few professionals line up slightly open, but their swing is on line. This open stance can sometimes help with a straighter backswing, promoting "straight back, straight through". It can sometimes improve line of sight from ball to target. The preferred method would be to line up squarely. The swing arc is slightly in-to-in, but it must still align with the target line.

It is recommended that the eyes be directly over the ball. Ideally, the nose should be in line with the ball and the eyes above the ball. The eyes must also be level. The head cannot be tilted. The ball will follow the eyes. If you raise your head before striking the putt, the eyes move from level and the ball will tend to follow the eyes. By keeping your eyes level the ball goes straight. Have you ever noticed that when you raised your head too soon you normally pushed the putt to the right, for a right handed golfer. The reason this occurred was because the arms and hands followed the eyes and everything shifted accordingly. Instead of thinking "keep your head down", you should think "keep your eyes level" until the ball is on its way. I've tried both thoughts and the eyes level serves a greater purpose and requires less thought.

Swing path is important for good putting. Ideally, if you could swing straight back and straight through, you would have superb accuracy. But our arms are attached to our shoulders and they are not in line with the ball when you swing. When you are bent over to putt, the short distance from the eyes to the shoulders will determine how much arc you will have when moving the club back and forth through the contact area. This arc is established by how you setup to the ball. Being square will encourage the arc being the same on both sides of the ball. The position of the ball is just as important as alignment. If the ball is too far forward, the ball will likely move more left. If the ball is too far back in the address, the ball will likely move more right. Your goal is to be centered. When the ball is struck, the contact needs to be at the center of the arc you established when you setup to the ball.

The putting stroke must have a relaxed tempo. A good tempo will have a specific rhythm based on your personality. The best putters use a One-Two count. One, moving the putter back, and two, striking the ball. The putting stoke should be back and through at the same pace. Think of a clock pendulum and you have the correct putting stroke. Then it is all about how fast the pendulum should move. Watch the pros on TV and count as they putt. Try to match their pace of One-Two when you practice. Be sure to count whenever you have a problem with your putting stroke. For some golfers counting can be used while playing on the course.

Even though your putting techniques may be excellent, you may still be just an average putter. If you misread the slope of the green and miss the putt, all the practicing will not produce the results you desire. There is a lot more involved for becoming a good putter. Reading greens can be a difficult quest. Some players just seem to have the ability to do this, while others struggle. Reading the green correctly will determine both aim point and distance. The factors to be considered are the type of grass, the direction of grain, the slope of the terrain, dryness of the turf, length of the turf, and sometimes even the wind.

Most greens are designed to control how water runs off the surface. They normally are sloped towards a water collection area and towards the fairway. Knowing this, a golfer should plan their approach shot to use the slope to improve their putting position. In other words, a good golfer should start reading a green a shot before the actual putt. After completing the approach shot, the slope of the green can be analyzed as the golfer walks to the green from the fairway. This is a great time to view the green because the slope is more apparent from a more distant view. Good players should decide ahead where the best position on the green is for making a putt.

Reading the slope once you are on the green is critical. This is because the slope will not only affect direction of travel, but also the speed the ball will travel. Since slope affects so much in how the ball will move, it is so important to understand how to better read the slope of the green. The slope must be read in the following ways. First, view from a distance as you approach the green. Next, study the green to judge to overall general slope and survey how the water would flow off its surface. The first two are the general slopes of the green. Then, crouch down behind the ball and study the slope to the left and right of the ball. If not sure about your read, walk to the opposite side of the hole and view the right and left slope. As you walk around the green try to feel the slope under your feet to get a better feel for the amount of slope.

After you have determined the slope, look for a line you think the ball should travel to the hole. Most good players visualize a spot about half the distance to the hole as the aim point. A downhill slope will make the ball travel faster. Therefore, the ball must be struck so the ball will travel slow enough to let gravity do most of the work. Downhill putts are difficult and the putt must be struck softly. A downhill putt will break a lot more than an uphill putt, so be careful not to underestimate the amount of break. Sidehill putts with a large amount of slope are always under read. So always play more than expected break since the ball will have to almost die at the hole. The reason uphill and downhill putts break differently is because of how gravity and friction work. On an uphill putt, the ball is struck harder but the energy of the ball is lost as it tries to climb the hill. With faster decreasing energy the ball will not move as much left or right. On a downhill putt, the ball has the additional energy of the slope, so the ball is struck lightly and the energy of the ball decreases slowly. Since the ball rolls out more from the slower decreasing energy, gravity has more time to progressively slow the ball. Therefore, the ball will have more time to turn left or right. As the ball starts to come to a stop, the break is more than when it was traveling faster at the start of the strike. Downhill putts can break 3 to 4 times more than uphill putts. Always play golf in such a way to avoid downhill putts. It is difficult for the individual to sense how gravity and friction work for downhill putts. Just keep in mind when you line up a downhill putt, play 10% more break than you expect and you will make more putts.

The turf on the green also affects speed and can affect how the ball breaks on slopes. The ball rolls faster on short cut greens. Therefore, the ball will break more on fast greens. Wet greens will produce more friction and slow down the ball. Dried out greens in the afternoon are faster than the greens in the morning. The grass on a green grows in numerous directions. If the grass is leaning towards you, it will be darker. If the grass is leaning away from you, it will appear shiny. The ball will roll faster down grain, which is shiny. If you have a long putt, this shiny or darker appearance will affect how fast the ball rolls.

Speed is so important for good putting. Remember, the slower the ball approaches the cup, the larger the hole. Gravity will help if the ball is moving slowly. The ball may often rim out if it is moving too fast. Ideally, putts should travel with a speed where the ball would go past the hole 12" to 18". Leaving the ball short on long putts is okay if it stops within a three foot radius. But remember the old adage, "never up, never in".

So how do you judge speed? After learning about all the things that have to be considered for making a putt, the answer to this question now seems more complex. What is needed, more than anything for answering this question, is "feel". It is amazing how our brains can perceive and do things that seem impossible to fathom. Astonishingly, how can the pros, more often than not, strike a ball 50 feet with a putter and come close to the hole almost every time? You can practice all day or until the cows come home and it won't do what the brain can do with little effort. Granted, practice does help, but still we are capable of so much that it is difficult to ascertain. If you relax, swing the putter with confidence, and let our experience control the mind, you can become a great putter.

Chapter 10

The Mental Side of Golf

" Golf is about how well you accept, respond to, and score with your misses much more so than it is a game of your perfect shots."

Dr. Bob Rotella

"It takes hundreds of good shots to gain confidence, but, only one bad one to lose it."

Jack Nicklaus

One of the best ways to reduce your score is to improve your mental approach to the game. The best players in the world are separated by one thing, how they handle "the mental side of golf". When Tiger Woods had a lead on the final day of a tournament, he rarely lost. The best golfers in the world know how to win under pressure.

Golf provides great moments of joy and then 10 minutes later, you feel like you've been punched in the stomach. And often, it may not have been the result of a poor swing or miscalculation. The ball just takes a bad bounce and erases everything you did well for almost an entire round. Golf can be brutal at times, showing no mercy. It is how you mentally handle the problems you face that can make the difference. The solution is normally to forget and move on. Every shot is a new shot. You cannot change the past.

Too many swing thoughts can be an immense problem for so many golfers. I can assure you, it can destroy your game. There is no drug you can take. There is no easy fix. There is only one solution – STOP DOING IT! This is easier said than done. After a while you become addicted, trying to fix your swing on the golf course. Under NO circumstances will this ever work. You have to realize, it never worked in the past, why do you expect it would in the future. Think for a moment, do you ever recall improving your score when you were constantly trying different swing thoughts every time you went out on the course? What might have worked one time, does not work the next. Why is this the case? I can tell you why. The right side of the brain is so confused that your brain basically short circuits. Confusion is not a good state of mind for golf. Mentally you need to be in a better place. You should just let go and play NATURAL golf. John Daley's motto is "grip and rip it". Having been one of the longest drivers of the ball for nearly a decade, you have to consider, maybe he had the right idea.

I am not saying swing thoughts are bad, but you must use them only when practicing. Earlier, I said to put all your swing thoughts into an empty pocket of your golf bag before removing a club. Let go, and have fun playing golf. Remember the name of the game is Golf, not Golf Swing.

How do you get rid of swing thoughts when playing a round of golf? And, at the same time remember all the swing techniques you have been practicing for weeks. To start, you have to develop a new way of perceiving just why you play golf in the first place. It's time to step back for a moment, and consider why you play this challenging game. Until you change your thinking about what you are trying to accomplish in golf, it may be an endless battle. I often play with guys that say "we are just out here to have fun". Rarely do they get upset. Funny thing, the more they play, the better they get. Many have never taken a lesson. Just think, if you took all that you know about golf and approached the game with their philosophy, I can't imagine the improvement, and without much effort. It's time to let go and trust that all your hard work will produce better results only by being relaxed and less serious. Once you let go of swing thoughts and constantly putting pressure on yourself, it may seem like the weight of the world has been lifted off your shoulders.

How to let go of swing thoughts requires Trust. It's time to trust what you have practiced, learned from lessons, and learned from playing. Trust requires all-out commitment. Every time you prepare to swing, you need to tell yourself, this is going to be a great shot. Tell yourself, "I know how to do this. I've done this before". Do your setup routine, and swing away. Swing with no regrets. If the swing was not your best, then accept and tell yourself you will do better the next time. It's time to begin having fun while playing golf. Other players may be watching, but they don't really care what you do. They are only thinking about their next shot. Just think about it, you really don't pay much attention to other players until you are all on the green. So why worry about anticipated results before you swing. There is no such thing as results until after you swing. The only thing you should think about is the target.

If you play target oriented golf, swing thoughts will take a back seat. Do you have swing thoughts when you swing a baseball bat? You are likely thinking "I'm going to hit the ball to left field". If you play target golf, you will naturally be more accurate. You will discover that your body will adapt and help make the swing needed to find your target. Another example, you are throwing a corn bag in a game of cornhole. You miss your target to the right of the hole. You don't change how you throw the bag to hit the target next time. You just focus harder on the target and let the body "do the rest". The human brain is amazing. You just need to relax and let nature take its course by letting the right side of the brain do its magic. We all have that magic. We are just not sure how to use it. You need to trust yourself. You must finally realize that the secret to playing better golf is not what you have been trying to orchestrate, but instead, it is already there inside you. If you TRUST what you already know and intensely focus on the target each time you setup to the ball, you will soon be a much better golfer.

Another way to avoid too many swing thoughts is confidence. Confidence is the holy grail for success in any sport, especially golf. So what is confidence and how do you achieve it? Confidence is defined as feeling sure of yourself and your own abilities. The only way to achieve this is to prepare yourself so well that you believe nothing can stop you from attaining your goal. If you have negative thoughts at any time on the golf course, before, during, and after a shot, you are doomed to failure. Doubt is your worst enemy. It will affect your thinking and produce excessive tension. Tight muscles do not swing a golf club. Most of the confident golfers I have seen are in total control, and appear so calm when they play. Pro golfers spent a lifetime building their confidence in golf. It is the result of constant training, practice, and accomplishment. So how does an amateur attain confidence without this degree of learning and achievement? Of course, you will never have the confidence of a pro, but instead it is about the level of play you aspire to. You cannot develop confidence if you constantly play with players that are extremely better than you. More importantly, it is tension and doubt that need to be avoided.

One of the best ways to develop confidence is to use a very structured routine during setup. This ritual is necessary to swing with a clear mind. The better you perform a routine, the more confidence you will have. Another way to instill confidence is to think only positive thoughts when playing. Learn to forget the bad shots, and move on. Always believe that the next shot will be your best shot. You can increase confidence with good planning. If you have a plan for how to play each hole, you will believe you have a better chance of scoring well. Plan ahead when playing. If you can land the ball on the green with an uphill putt remaining, you can be confident you will make the putt. Building confidence is just that. You have to <u>build</u> it one step at a time. The greater your confidence, the better you will score.

You're standing over the ball and there is a lake on the right and thick woods on the left. How do you block negative thoughts out of your mind? Focus on the basics you have learned, not hazards. It is all about better focus. Remember the example of throwing the cornhole bag. What is needed is very deliberate focus. You can never focus too much. Very few amateur golfers are good at deep concentration or focus when setting up to strike the ball. But, if you were about to fire a gun, your aim becomes so intense you can feel it throughout your body. The pros can focus so intently that they can block out the mass hysteria that takes place with the fans and TV coverage. Some sports analysts call it the "quiet eye". The look in the eyes of pros as they prepare to strike the ball is so intense you can sense they are in total control of that moment. The amateur can learn to focus better. Good focus requires calmness in the thought pattern. This calmness is the result of believing in oneself. You are extremely committed to the actions you are about to perform. There can be no doubt about the task at hand. You can practice being more focused by thinking about things you have done in the past that required intense focus. Good focus requires more than just the eyes. You need the whole body to be committed to the effort. This includes all your senses and every part of your being. This type of deep mental thought is common to all martial arts, why not golf.

Better focus can also be the result of a good setup routine and visualizing the shot in your mind before you start the swing. With this good focus you are swinging with blinders on. You will not see the lake on the right or the woods on the left. You only see the ball flying to the target you chose during the setup routine. When visualizing a target be very specific. This helps your concentration as well. If you are throwing darts, you look at the smallest target in the middle. This requires very intense focus. If you are hitting a shot to the green, pick at small target in the background as your target. First get the aim correct and the distance is determined by choosing the correct club. When the media focus microphones on the pros, you can hear them talking with their caddie. They might say "I'll aim for the pole on the TV tower". Or, "I'll aim for the "L" on the sign". For the amateur, detailed targets can also prevent thinking about negative thoughts before swinging. Next time you are on a par 3 hole, focus intently on a spot on the green or a branch of a tree behind the green. Be very specific. This will require deep concentration and this should help eliminate distractions or negative thoughts.

Visualization is important for many reasons. Jack Nicklaus excelled in this part of the swing. He mentions in his book, "Golf My Way" that he had the ability to see in his mind a movie of the ball in flight, and land on the green where he desired. All this happens before the club begins to move. By simply replaying the movie in his mind, his body would do what was necessary to make the preplanned shot happen. Once you learn how to use a focus technique that works for you, your game will become less stressful and you will be surprised how your score improves.

To develop a swing image for mental recall, use golf videos. Watch the videos many times, then close your eyes and try to remember every detail. This will help you learn the process of imaging in your mind. Next, imagine you are setting up for a shot on a particular hole at the course you play. You know the hole well, so it is easy to imagine yourself there in that place. Start by imagining yourself setting up to the ball and going through your entire routine. Include every little detail.

Make it a movie. Then watch yourself swing. Include a good takeaway and a nice finish position. Visualize the ball coming off the clubhead and watch it travel to the point you chose in the setup routine. The more detail the better. Do this imaging many times and for several holes and you will eventually be a master at visualization. I would suggest choosing one hole that has been your nemesis hole every time you play. This particular hole is like there are demons lurking, causing you to hit a bad shot every time. If you can overcome this sorcery, by removing the spell with visualization, you will have passed the test, and be on your way to better golf.

So you just hit a bad shot and the ball travels deep into the woods. You are so mad that you slam the club into the ground with frustrated anger. You think your entire round is about to be destroyed. You find your ball and you are still upset and it's hard to make a rational decision. Finally, you grab a club in hast, and swing wildly to get the ball out of the thick brush. It moves maybe 2 feet and you are ready to give up. One hole has ruined the entire round. Does this sound familiar? What should you have been done in this case? Accept the consequences, take a penalty stroke or retee the ball, forget the bad shot, and move on. Never let one bad shot ruin your day. This game is supposed provide enjoyment, not persecution. Again, it's a game! Every shot is a new beginning. Your next shot will be a great shot! Only if you remove the negative thoughts that tend to accumulate will you be able to perform at your highest level. Just follow your normal routine and think only about your immediate target and you will keep the negative thoughts at bay. As long as you think about the good shots you made so far in the round, you will tend to forget the bad ones. Stay positive even when you're having a bad day.

Another mental approach to improve your game is good planning. This part of the game can save a lot of strokes. One of the most consequential is underclubbing. For amateurs, I would guess that 90 percent of approach shots stop short of the green by 10 to 15 yards: one club short. Next time you can't decide what club to use, go with the longer club. I know, if you hit the ball perfectly, it may be over the green. How often do you hit a perfect shot? Even the great Ben Hogan said he hit only 3 or 4 "perfect" shots per round.

Amateurs make decisions as if they were a pro. If you know a shot would be a challenge for a pro player, definitely choose a conservative approach. This decision will always prevent a high score on a specific hole. Know your limitations. The results are almost always better when taking a conservative approach. If a hole has water or thick rough, choose a club that provides confidence. The driver may have to stay in the bag. Taking risks should be avoided whenever possible. For amateurs, the odds of being successful with a shot that would be difficult for a professional, are almost zero. If you have a hole that is very challenging, avoid being aggressive. Sometimes it is better to lay up safe, providing an easy wedge shot to the green. Even pro golfers try to avoid risky shots. It is better to choose clubs that provide more confidence when faced with a stressful shot. You can even choke down on the grip or swing easier with a favorite club.

Just like pool, a golfer should plan one shot ahead. Your target should always provide an easier opportunity for the next shot. This is especially important if there are hazards. If you do not think about the best landing spot for the next shot, you will often be faced with a difficult shot rather than an easy one. If there are bunkers or any hazards, choose the right club to avoid them. Most amateurs do not plan ahead. Ben Hogan would often walk the course backwards just to get a better perspective on how to approach each green. Plan ahead for success.

In conclusion, "Golf is a complicated sport but you play your best when you are not thinking." Larry Eichenauer

Epilogue

"The real way to enjoy playing golf is to take pleasure not in the score, but in the execution of the strokes."

Bobby Jones

"Success in golf is less on strength of body than upon strength of mind and character."

Arnold Palmer

There are 5 things that stand out, which I will call game changers for amateurs. There is no particular order of importance.

(1) Swing tempo. For years I tried to reduce the pace of my backswing. This was the biggest mistake I made in my effort to improve my swing. I had no idea how much this affects timing. It destroyed my game. Nearly all the pros have a smooth somewhat quick backswing. There has to be a reason for this. Most pros have a 3 to 1 ratio, .75 seconds back, .25 seconds down to impact. If you can get close to these numbers, your swing will be so much better. There are always exceptions, but generally speaking, this is a key move.

(2) Takeaway. Jack Nicklaus said this is the most important part of the golf swing. He may be right. It takes a while to understand the move that the best golfers make as they start their swing. Once I figured it out, it all became clear to me. By moving the shoulders, arms, and hands together around the center core of your body, it sets up everything properly for the rest of the swing. The key to this move was the "rotation around the core". If you do this move correctly, you can feel the movement near what I called the "dan-tien". It will feel like

entire body is in full control as you make the takeaway move.

(3) Right brain vs. Left brain. Once I understood how the brain works for creating movement, it became clear why swing thoughts were killing my game. Swing thoughts were creating confusion. If you want to have total freedom in a golf swing, you cannot think about it.

(4) Focus. The better the focus, the better the shot. I never realized how important this was until I learned how to concentrate while swinging a golf club. I had to relate to other sports, wherein I did focus intently, to understand that I was not doing this when golfing. I let distractions control the swing. Good focus and visualization are the best methods to eliminate negative thoughts and swing thoughts.

(5) How to Practice. All the years I went to the range, hitting balls until I was exhausted, practicing new swing thoughts each time, and making little progress. Finally, I started using slow motion drills at home for each important segment of the golf swing. Swing thoughts transformed into natural motions. This entirely changed how I practiced. Every shot at the range now has a purpose.

"The ultimate judge of your swing

is the flight of the ball."

Ben Hogan

Acknowledgements

There were several books that provided some of the quotes and thoughts in the text of this book. "Golf My Way" by Jack Nicklaus. "Ben Hogan's Secret Fundamental" by Larry Miller. "Five Lessons-The Modern Fundamentals of Golf" by Ben Hogan.

Quotations at the beginning of each chapter were obtained on-line from three sources: Golf Digest.com, Kidadl.com, and Southern California Golf Association (scga.com)

All Photos: istockphoto.com
Front Cover - floridastock
Back Cover - VasjaKoman
Fig. 1 - Michael Svoboda, Fig. 2 - nattrass, Fig. 3 - 4x6, Fig. 4 - af_istocker, Fig. 5 - nattrass, Fig. 6 - stockstudioX, Fig. 7 - OSTILL, Fig. 8 - THACHKORN_TJ, Fig. 9 - OtmarW

www.ingramcontent.com/pod-product-compliance
Lightning Source LLC
Chambersburg PA
CBHW051537120626
46551CB00013B/1264